DESTINY
ENCOUNTER

DESTINY ENCOUNTER

APOSTLE FRITZ TAKANG

XULON PRESS

Xulon Press
2301 Lucien Way #415
Maitland, FL 32751
407.339.4217
www.xulonpress.com

© 2017 by Apostle Fritz Takang

Edited by Xulon Press.

Unless otherwise indicated, Scripture quotations
taken from the King James Version (KJV)–
public domain.

Printed in the United States of America.

ISBN-13: 9781545617328

Table of Contents

Introduction

Mountains are so impressive and huge that a passerby cannot ignore the beauty of its shape, but it's impossible to transport the physical appearance of the structure except in the mind of the beholder. It is said, "if you have faith like that of a mustard seed, you can say to a mountain, 'be thou removed,' and it will be removed" (Matthew 17:6). "How beautiful are the feet of they who preach the gospel of peace and bring glad tidings of good things" (Romans 10:15b). Humans have feet to move and are always on motion.

Destiny encounter involves everyone who loves God and is willing to transform his or her mind every day as we face the motions of life. Mount Fako in Buea is a monumental picture that remains in our mind for some of us who spend our teenage life in the western part of the Cameroons, together with visitors who come in from all over the world to partake in the Guinness Mount Cameroon race in the present southwest region. Both indigenes and visitors come in and out, but that gigantic structure never fades in the mind.

The person you neglect on your way up the mountain might be the one you need when on the way coming back down the mountain because everything that goes up will still come down and that which goes around will still come around. Life is like a cycle, but directed by the invisible hand of God according to time and seasons as touching our destiny. The mind is a great reservoir that keeps impressions stored on it once and forever. The mind must be set and fashioned in such a way that will produce not only positive memories, but good effects in our day to day encounters with people and events.

Genesis 24: 1-67

Long gone from home after hearing the voice of God inviting him to a land of promise, living behind kindred's, and all that was in his father's house to settle in a distant land where the blessings attached to the invitation where manifested, then came the need to go back home by delegation for the sake of necessity. This is a love story, a story of destiny encounter. It is a kind of manual that tells us what to do and how to go about preparing ourselves to enter the stage in every endeavor of life. Abraham calls the main servant of his house and gives him instruction on matters concerning the choice of wife he wants for his son, Isaac.

He made him to swear an oath and provided him with a kind of open check in to his treasures so that he had enough to embark in the journey to search and bring back home a ventures woman for his son Isaac.

Chapter One

Mindset of
Destiny Encounter

W e were in a company of four going
to make an enquiry around the
neighborhood in regards to my cousin,
Prince. Suddenly Pastor Bethania calls
out to sister Rosanna, "Look who is
coming," and it was Mauro, a longtime
member of the church who left without
any notification.

Conversation began and it resulted
that my cousin Prince was neighbor
to Mauro. Prince and I had lost sight
of each other for more than a decade

because of the bad socioeconomic and political unrest in Cameroon, the continent of Africa, which have made many youths — especially from the English speaking regions — to abdicate from the country to seek refuge and greener pasture far from home.

In this adventure of search, youths go through the Sahara desert, passing mountains, hills, and valleys under hideous atmospheric conditions, risking their lives in the Mediterranean Sea and sometimes, many die without fulfilling the dream of a better life.

Most often, you are not sure who will survive and who will make it though this journey.

One beautiful Sunday morning, my mother who was visiting from the United States of America, and I visited an African Nigerian oriented church in the city of Vercelli, Italy. There in the congregation was my cousin Prince seated without us knowing. Only to see him turn up at the end of the service to greet us and introduce himself to us. This was special because I came to this city to open a mission center for Tabernacle Foundation International and I never expected to find anybody I knew previously. This was an indication to me that God is able to place people on our way we never expected to be our destiny helpers in the part of destiny encounter. Sometimes life is like a film well planed beforehand just to be played on stage. That is why principles are to be respected so as to face and get the best out of every situation and circumstances that come our way.

In the same manner, we went out to check on Prince few months later in the company of Pastor Bethania and sister Rossana, and behold, Mauro comes out. As we stood there to contemplate this as not just a coincidence, it dawned on me that it was an encounter of destiny. We went out to see the house in which Prince was living so as to keep in touch and have him be part of my new project in the city. This brought us to meet new people with whom I was able to explain our mission and desire to have them become part of our community. The visit became an opportunity to preach the Gospel to those who were in the neighborhood.

There is no causality for encounters of destiny because they are designed and programmed by God for the purpose of profitability for those involved and for the kingdom of God.

The Word of God's address to Jeremiah for the people of God reads:

"For I know the thoughts that I think towards you," saith the Lord, "thoughts of peace and not of Evil, to give you an expected end. Then shall ye call upon me, and ye shall go and pray unto me, and I will hearken unto you. And ye shall seek me, and find me, when ye shall search for me with all your heart. And I will be found of you," saith the Lord: "and I will turn away your captivity." (Jeremiah 29:11-14)

God is forever present in the affairs of men since the beginning of all creation. That is why He is omnipresent. This is the attribute of God in which He fills the universe in all its parts and is present everywhere at once. The whole of God, not just a part of Him, is present in every place. He acts to fulfill His purpose of granting unto man welfare and satisfaction so that mankind understands that we are not alone in the cycle of life, which destiny encounter plays a great role.

We also call Him omnipotent in that He fights and defends us even when we don't see the warfare. Omnipotence is the attribute that describes God's ability to do whatever He wills. God's will is limited by His nature. He cannot do anything that is contrary to His perfect nature. God cannot lie (Titus 1:2). God cannot destroy (deny) Himself (2 Timothy 2:13). God cannot look with favor on iniquity. God cannot do wrong (1 Peter 4:17). God cannot do anything that is absurd (foolish) or self-contradictory, such as make a square a circle, make two plus two equal six, or make a wrong right.

God is not controlled by His power; the existence of omnipotence does not demand the exercise of that power. He has power over His power, or else He would cease to be free. He can do what He wills, but He does not have to will to do anything.

Omnipotence includes the power of self-limitation. God limited Himself to some extent by giving free will to His creatures. This is why He did not keep sin out of the universe by a display of His power and why He does not save anyone by force, or impose destiny encounters.

God is omniscient, which means He knows everything in the present, past, and future. God knows Himself and all other things perfectly from all eternity, whether they are actual or merely possible. They alone (the Father, Son, and Holy Spirit) have such knowledge of each other (Matthew 11:27; 1 Corinthians 2:11). God knows the things that are actually existing, including inanimate creation (Psalm 147:4), men and all their works (Psalm 33:13-15), men's thoughts and hearts (Psalm 139:1-4), and man's burdens and wants (Exodus 3:7; Matthew 6:8).

God knows all things that are possible (1 Samuel 23:11; Matthew 11:23). God knows the future. Foreknowledge is not causative; future actions do not take place because they are known, but they are seen/known because they will take place. God knows simultaneously; He sees things at once in their totality, one after another, and not piecemeal.

God is omniscient such that His intelligence cannot be measured. He makes everything beautiful in its appointed time.

For any encounter of destiny to have an outcome of profitability, the mindset of destiny encounter must be established in the fabrics of our entire being: body, soul, and spirit. When we accept God's existence as Him being the designer of our life as the potter and we being the clay, we must also accept the fact that even the minor details of our lives are also in the part of his agenda and our lives are to be framed according to destiny encounters designed by the almighty God.

Chapter Two

The Mindset of Rules and Regulations (Law)

As we know, the book of Genesis contains four different dispensation or periods according to God's calendar with humans and the entire universe. These dispensations are the pre-Adamic dispensation, the dispensation of innocence, the dispensation of human conscience, and that of human governments.

Our story is situated in the time when man was under God's calendar according to the dispensation of human government.

It's important to note that besides the above-mentioned four dispensations, there are three other dispensations including the one we are living in at this moment. The dispensation of the law, that of grace, which is the current dispensation, and that of the millennium.

Our storyline is written under the dispensation of the law but took place under the dispensation of human governments, which is before the law.

The protagonist and the different characters of the narrative lived under the dispensation of the human government, but the writer wrote from the standpoint of the dispensation of the law (Moses). While we are interpreting from the standpoint of the dispensation of grace (from death to ascension of Christ) including His return and rapture. Then will begin the dispensation of the millennial reign of Christ, according to eschatological teachings.

> And Abraham was old, and well stricken in age: and the Lord had blessed Abraham in all things. And Abraham said unto his eldest servant of his house, that ruled over all that he had, "Put, I pray thee, thy hand under my thigh: And I will make thee swear by the Lord, the God of heaven, and the God of the earth, that thou shall not take a wife unto my son of the daughters of the Canaanites, among whom I dwell: But thou shall go unto my country, and to my kindred, and take a wife unto my son Isaac." And the servant said unto him, "Peradventure the woman will not be willing

to follow me unto this land: must I needs bring thy son again unto the land from whence thou camest?" And Abraham said unto him, "Beware thou that thou bring not my son thither again. The Lord God of heaven, which took me from my father's house, and from the land of my kindred, and which spoke unto me, and that swore unto me, saying, 'Unto thy seed will I give this land;' he shall send his angel before thee, and thou shall take a wife unto my son from thence. And if the woman will not be willing to follow thee, then thou shall be clear from this my oath: only bring not my son thither again." The servant put his hand under the thigh of Abraham his master, and swore to him concerning that matter (Genesis 24:1-9)

Typology

We will be considering the image of Abraham as the father of faith in the position of God, the creator of heaven and earth, and Eliezer as the chosen servant appointed to execute the pleasure of the father, which is to bring home the bride of the son.

In this capacity we can consider the servant in the person of Eliezer as the representation of the Holy Spirit.

While the image of Isaac as the beloved son of the father to be the image of Christ, and on the other hand, the bride in the person of Rebecca, which is the representation of the church still in the world waiting for liberation and to be accepted yet into the household of the master.

The name of Rebecca gives us deep insight to her image. The name Rebecca means, "to clog by tying the fetlock," which is a chain by which a person or an animal is confined by the foot.

Eliezer, which also denotes God's help or helper, is a type of the Holy Spirit whom the father sends to help the believer to fulfill the Father's will.

"Likewise the Spirit also helpeth our infirmities: for we know not what we should pray for as we ought: but the Spirit itself maketh intercession for us with groanings which cannot be uttered." (Romans 8:26)

"Let your conversation be without covetousness; and be content with such things as ye have: for he hath said, 'I will never leave thee, nor forsake thee.'" (Hebrews 13:5)

"So that we may boldly say, 'The Lord is my helper, and I will not fear what man shall do unto me.'" (Hebrews 13:6)

The universe is governed by rules and regulations (laws). These apply to all aspects of life, be it in the society, the family or the church. We are therefore obligated to master the rules and the regulations so as to benefit from any destiny encounter and live a well-fulfilled life of happiness in God's presence and blessings.

Everyone involved in God's call of destiny must master the rules and regulations that govern the area of profitability in the encounter of destiny.

It is written:

"And I will give unto thee the keys of the kingdom of Heaven: and whatsoever thou shall bind on earth shall be bound in heaven: and whatsoever thou shall loose on earth shall be loosed in heaven." (Matthew 16:19)

The earth is just a replica of heaven, which is why we are to pray in this manner: "Let thy will be done on earth as it is in heaven" (Matthew 6:10). If you bind here, it is bound there, and if you lose here, it is loosed there.

"No man can enter into a strong man's house, and spoil his goods, except he will first bind the strong man; and then he will spoil his house." (Mark 3:27)

The name of Rebecca means, "one who is bound with a chain," yet is the supposed wife of the one called laughter (Isaac). She was beautiful but not married; she was related to Abraham but far in Mesopotamia locked up in the pagan world, staying with Laban, the fetish priest who was his brother.

So is the case of many creatures of God living in our present world — lovely people, relatives, and friends living in this world having no hope and future because they are void of the grace and presence of God in their life. Having a feeling of a better life, but no power to take hold of true peace and love, surrounded in a world of occultism and fetish practices.

In order to get Rebecca in line to a destiny encounter, the rule of engagement had to come in to place (the mindset of rules and regulations, which is important to align to the will of a loving father who has everything and is willing to give the best to his children).

This is represented by the swearing of an oath. Abraham, the master, was not under the dispensation of the law, but understood rules and regulation are keys for orderliness and are profitable for those who build a mindset to apply them.

The journey was from the Middle East to Asia Minor and the mission was to bring back home a bride for the groom, symbolic for the work of the Holy Spirit whom the father has sent to convict us of this sinful world and win us to the Son of God in the person of Jesus Christ, the groom, or the husband of the church, which is also called His body.

Rule of Engagement
Oath
An oath is a solemn affirmation or declaration, made with an appeal to God

for the truth of what is affirmed. Many of us have not taken an affirmation for the truth in every cycle of life; be it social, labor, educational, or family, there is the need of affirmation and a sense of belonging. Sometimes you hear people say, "I am with you," but there is no sign of engagement because their heart is far.

For a medical doctor to practice medicine or a lawyer to get in to activity, they must swear an oath.

If we will go far in this life, we must build a mindset of affirmation to the truth of what we believe in.

An affirmation, which is an oath in form of a declaration, will enable us to go far in the encounter of destiny — be it in carrier, marriage, or family.

I believe in you. I believe in my job. I believe in the Word of God. I believe in my leader. Simple affirmations can carry you a long way.

Lack of affirmation can hinder you from going far; we are encouraged by the Word of God to be people of our word.

By taking an oath to Abraham, Eliezer identified himself to his master and to the God of his master. The fact that he has been a servant for many years and won the place of the eldest servant does not guarantee him to take the journey without an oath.

The specific destiny encounter here was touching marriage and the values that go with it.

Being an institution ordained by God, all the rules of engagement and affirmation have to be put into play. Abraham already laid down what will become the rules to follow in regards to what will become a pattern for believers' marriage.

In the book of Leviticus, strange practices were carried out by pagans as far back as Sodom and Gomorrah and light is giving unto us in chapter eighteen of Leviticus.

The doings of the land of Egypt:
They uncover the nakedness of near kin.
They slept with their fathers and mother.
They slept with brothers and sisters, including in-laws.
They slept with aunties and uncles.
They took their brother's wife.
They took the wife of their neighbors.
They took their wives' sisters and their wives' daughters.
They slept with women in time of menstruation.
The doings of the land of Canaan:
They offer their unwanted babies to Moloch by fire.

They slept man with man (homosexuality). They slept women with women (lesbianism).

They had sexual pleasure with animals (bestiality).

> After the doings of the land of Egypt, wherein ye dwelt, shall ye not do: and after the doings of the land of Canaan, whither I bring you, shall ye not do: neither shall ye walk in their ordinances. Ye shall do my judgments, and keep mine ordinances, to walk therein: I am the Lord your God. Ye shall therefore keep my statutes, and my judgments: which if a man do, he shall live in them: I am the Lord. None of you shall approach to any that is near of kin to him, to uncover their nakedness: I am

the Lord. The nakedness of thy father, or the nakedness of thy mother, shall thou not uncover: she is thy mother; thou shall not uncover her nakedness. The nakedness of thy father's wife shall thou not uncover: it is thy father's nakedness. The nakedness of thy sister, the daughter of thy father, or daughter of thy mother, whether she be born at home, or born abroad, even their nakedness thou shall not uncover. The nakedness of thy son's daughter, or of thy daughter's daughter, even their nakedness thou shall not uncover: for theirs is thin own nakedness. The nakedness of thy father's wife's daughter, begotten of thy father, she is thy sister; thou shall not uncover her nakedness. Thou shall not uncover the nakedness of thy father's sister: she is thy father's near kinswoman. Thou shall not uncover the nakedness of thy mother's sister: for she is thy mother's near kinswoman. Thou shall not uncover the nakedness of thy father's brother; thou shall not approach to his wife: she is thin aunt. Thou shall not uncover the nakedness of thy daughter in law: she is thy son's wife; thou shall not uncover her nakedness. Thou shall not uncover the nakedness of thy brother's wife: it is thy brother's nakedness. Thou shall not uncover the nakedness of a woman and her daughter; neither shall thou take her son's daughter, or her daughter's daughter, to uncover her nakedness; for they are her near kinswomen: it is wickedness. Neither shall thou take a wife to her sister, to vex her, to uncover her nakedness, beside the other in her lifetime. Also thou shall not approach unto a woman to uncover her nakedness, as long as she is put apart for her uncleanness. Moreover thou shall not lie carnally with thy neighbor's wife, to defile thyself with her. And thou shall not let any of thy seed pass through the fire to Moloch; neither shall thou profane the name of thy God: I am the Lord. Thou shall not lie with mankind, as with womankind: it is abomination. Neither shall thou lie with any beast to defile thyself therewith: neither shall any woman stand before a beast to lie down thereto: it is confusion. Defile not ye yourselves in any of these things: for in all these the nations are defiled which I cast out before you: And the land is defiled: therefore I do visit the iniquity thereof upon it, and the land itself vomited out her inhabitants. Ye shall therefore keep my statutes and my judgments, and shall not commit any of these abominations; neither any of your own nation, nor any stranger that sojourned among you: (For all these abominations have the men of the land done, which were before you, and the land is defiled) That the land spud not you out also, when ye defile it, as it spud out the nations that were before you. For whosoever shall commit any of these abominations, even the souls that commit them shall be cut off from among their people Therefore shall ye keep mine ordinance, that ye commit not any one of these abominable customs, which were committed before you, and that ye defile not yourselves therein: I am the Lord your God. (Leviticus 18:3-30)

As against this above mention practices, there was need for an oath to be taken by the servant of Abraham whose name signifies "my God is help" (Eliezer). We need help from God in this present

generation against incest, against homosexuality, against bestiality and adultery.
The same challenges of the ancient time
are what we see today going on in the
modern world: incest, adultery, homosexuality, and bestiality are destroying
marriages and destabilizing families
and entire communities and nations.
For these reasons, we have to play by
the rules and build a strong mindset of
rules and regulations in taking a stand
upon our declaration of faith.

We are much closer to the end of this
dispensation of grace, and the bride of
Christ still in the world is waiting for us
to come by the leadership of the Holy
Spirit and loose her from the chains of
ungodliness.

The bride is waiting for us to take
the oath and come deliver her from
the prince of the air who has taken her

captive, like Rebecca with chains on her legs, but innocent of the devices of the wicked one.

The practices and lifestyle of Egypt and Canaan was not strange to Abraham; he understood the dynamics of pairing with a close relative; in fact, married to Sarah as his half-sister was not the perfect will of God. The delay of child-bearing was not casual as we consider the period of his call at the age of seventy-five and only at age 100 that he could get a child, which is by the spirit through the prophecy of the Lord by the destiny encounter of the three angels.

"Is anything too hard for the Lord? At the time appointed I will return unto thee, according to the time of life, and Sarah shall have a son." (Genesis 18:14)

If we consider he was forty when he was married, then it took sixty years for him to be able to have a child, most of his kin had children at the age of thirty. Examples of the following in line for generations from his father by name Nahor:

And Peleg lived thirty years, and begat Reu: And Peleg lived after he begat Reu two hundred and nine years, and begat sons and daughters. And Reu lived two and thirty years, and begat Serug: And Reu lived after he begat Serug two hundred and seven years, and begat sons and daughters. And Serug lived thirty years, and begat Nahor: And Serug lived after he begat Nahor two hundred years, and begat sons and daughters. And Nahor lived nine and twenty years, and begat Terah: And Nahor lived after he begat

Terah a hundred and Abraham understood the absent of the rule of law and was afraid to the point of living in half truth so as to preserve his life because the revelation of God for him was still in progression. (Genesis 11:18-25)

"And Abraham said, 'Because I thought, surely the fear of God is not in this place; and they will slay me for my wife's sake.'" (Genesis 20:11)

"And yet indeed she is my sister; she is the daughter of my father, but not the daughter of my mother; and she became my wife." (Genesis 20:12)

The Damaging Effect of Homosexuality

The Homosexual Rape of Lot's Guests

The Hebrew verb ידע (*yada*), translated as "know" in the King James Version: "And they called unto Lot, and said unto him, 'Where [are] the men which came in to thee this night? Bring them out unto us, that we may know them'" (Genesis 19:5).

However, the word "know" in the King James Version has been used as referring to sexual intercourse. One example can be found in Genesis 4:1 between Adam and Eve: "And Adam knew Eve his wife; and she conceived, and bare Cain, and said, 'I have gotten a man from the Lord.'"

Some Hebrew scholars believe *yada*, unlike the English word "know" requires the existence of a "personal and intimate relationship." For this reason, many of the most popular of the twentieth century translations, including the New International Version, the New King James Version, and the New Living Translation, translate *yada* as "have sex with" or "know ... carnally" in Genesis 19:5.

> And Lot went up out of Zoar, and dwelt in the mountain and his two daughters with him; for he feared to dwell in Zoar: and he dwelt in a cave, he and his two daughters. And the firstborn said unto the younger, "Our father is old, and there is not a man in the earth to come in unto us after the manner of all the earth: Come, let us make our father drink wine, and we will lie with him, that we may preserve seed of our father." And they made their father drink wine that night:

and the firstborn went in, and lay with her father; and he perceived not when she lay down, nor when she arose. And it came to pass on the morrow, that the firstborn said unto the younger, "Behold, I lay yester night with my father: let us make him drink wine this night also; and go thou in, and lie with him, that we may preserve seed of our father." And they made their father drink wine that night also: and the younger arose, and lay with him; and he perceived not when she lay down, nor when she arose. Thus were both the daughters of Lot with child by their father. And the firstborn bare a son, and called his name Moab: the same is the father of the Moabites unto this day. And the younger, she also bare a son, and called hisname Benammi: the same is the father of the children of Ammon unto this day. (Genesis 19:30-38)

Over the news in our radios, television, and newspapers, we read of fathers sleeping with their daughters, men going after men, women going after women, and humans having sexual pleasure with animals. The church sits quiet and says it's normal instincts — no, that's the nature of both Canaan and Egypt in the time of Abraham taking place in our modern day world.

The aftermath of Babel was outright confusion not only in the atmosphere, but in the way family units were organized. For example, in Genesis chapter eleven, the family structures of Terah, the father of Abraham, whose wife was not mentioned except by the writings of tradition, states as follows:

> Genesis 11:27: "Now these are the generations of Terah: Terah begat Abram, Nahor, and Haran; and Haran begat Lot."

> Genesis 11:28: "And Haran died before his father Terah in the land of his nativity, in Ur of the Chaldees."

> Genesis 11:29: "And Abram and Nahor took them wives: the name of Abram's wife was Sarai; and the name of Nahor's wife, Milcah, the daughter of Haran, the father of Milcah, and the father of Iscah."

> Genesis 11:30: "But Sarai was barren; she had no child."

Genesis 11:31: "And Terah took Abram his son, and Lot the son of Haran his son's son, and Sarai his daughter in law, his son Abram's wife; and they went forth with them from Ur of the Chaldees, to go into the land of Canaan; and they came unto Haran, and dwelt there."

Terah

First wife mother to the three sons Second wife mother to sarah	Sarah Daughter	Lot slept two Daughter s
Haran Father of Lot Milcah and Iscah	Nahor uncle and husband to Milcah who bore Bethuel father to laban and rebecca .	Abraham

The family structure demonstrates polygamy and incest at its core, which implies grace was to manifest to bring

Abraham out for the power of God to be demonstrated in his life.

> Genesis 12:1: "Now the Lord had said unto Abram, 'Get thee out of thy country, and from thy kindred, and from thy father's house, unto a land that I will show thee.'"

> Genesis 12:2: "And I will make of thee a great nation, and I will bless thee, and make thy name great; and thou shall be a blessing."

> Genesis 12:3: "And I will bless them that bless thee, and curse him that curses thee: and in thee shall all families of the earth be blessed."

Abraham got married to his own half-sister as seen in Genesis 20:12: "And yet indeed she is my sister; she is the daughter of my father, but not the daughter of my mother; and she became my wife."

Ebn Batrik, in his analysis, among other ancient traditions, has preserved the following: "Terah first married Yona, by whom he had Abraham; afterwards he married Tehevita, by whom he had Sarah."

Abraham is coming from a deep chaotic and confused family setup and that is the reason the call of God for him was strong.

The journey to bring home the bride, an encounter of destiny, was a long one just as the heavens are far from the earth; we need the help of God to get through this present life and all its corrupt practices so as to be effective in the art of soul-winning. With the help of God, we shall overcome through the affirmation of our faith by the love of God in our heart.

The mindset of rules will open the door for everyday encounters of destiny. The father of multitude calls on God's help to come take the engagement for the journey to bring home the bride for laughter to flow in abundance. As we affirm our rules and regulations in the faith, our deliverance is sure.

The mindset of rules and regulations intends that we up hold a sound society by accepting God's plan for a better life.

It is wrong to have sexual intercourse with close relatives.

It is wrong to have man-to-man or woman-to-woman sexual relationships.

It is wrong to have fun or pleasure with animals.

It is wrong to commit abortion.

It is wrong to take a neighbor's wife.

Bring back rules and regulations to our educational system and our society will be a better place with people fulfilling their purpose and entering into their destiny encounters as ordered by God.

When rules and regulations are applied in the institutions of the state, eventually sound, moral standards are kept and people's character become more religiously inclined and this leads to more awareness of the presence of God, thus bringing about the formation of the mindset of godly character.

Chapter Three

The Mindset of
Godly Character

Genesis 24:10: "And the servant took ten camels of the camels of his master, and departed; for all the goods of his master were in his hand: and he arose, and went to Mesopotamia, unto the city of Nahor."

For any destiny encounter to be profitable for God, there must be the elements of godly character. Godly character is the only medicine to heal the world that is perishing in lust and self-gratification. In fact, to this wicked and dark world, we need light to walk through and a strong force of character, which will be seen in the number of camels Eliezer will take to embark from Canaan to Mesopotamia.

Ten is the number of the law and signifies light.

Jesus is the light of the world, and Jesus is the end of the law.

Proverbs 6:23-25: "For the commandment is a lamp; and the law is light; and reproofs of instruction are the way of life: To keep thee from the evil woman, from the flattery of the tongue of a strange woman. Lust not after her beauty in thin heart; neither let her take."

The animal used for the journey was none other than camels.

The Camel's Life

Camels are social animals that roam the deserts in search of food and water, with up to thirty other animals. With the exception of rutting males competing for females, camels are peaceful animals that rarely exhibit aggression.

Contrary to popular misconception, camels do not store water in their humps; the humps are actually reservoirs for fatty tissue. Concentrating fat in their humps minimizes insulation throughout the rest of the body, thus allowing camels to survive in extremely hot regions.

Asian camels have two humps, whereas Arabian camels only have one.

Camels have two rows of thick eyelashes to protect their eyes from the desert dust. They are also able to close their nostrils and lips to keep out the dust.

Camels' ears are small and hairy; however, their sense of hearing is also extremely strong.

The amount of water a camel drinks on a day-to-day basis can vary greatly, as they drink to replace only the fluid they've lost throughout the day. A thirsty camel can drink up to 135 liters in one sitting.

In Arab cultures, the camel symbolizes patience, tolerance, and endurance.

Matthew 19:24: And again I say unto you, it is easier for a camel to go through the eye of a needle, than for a rich man to enter into the kingdom of God.

Elements of Godly Character

Characteristics of camels bring out great elements of godly character, which are patience, tolerance, endurance, and humility. A camel travels forty kilometers a day at a speed of five kilometers per hour. It is able to carry one hundred to four hundred and fifty kilograms of load, stand tall about 1.8 to two meters and weigh about 250 to 680 kilograms. It is the most sociable beast and the most domesticated of all beasts. Camels will always go down on their knees to carry a load, which is a great sign of humility. It's an animal that travels long distances on desert land with little food or water and walks on sand without being stuck. Camels endure harsh desert climates and have patience to go long distances. They also tolerate aggression from both humans and other beasts. Camels go beyond twelve months of conception and bring forth at thirteenth month of pregnancy.

Forty speaks of maturity, five speaks of grace. The choice of a woman to be brought back home was to be mature and gracious. Five also represents ministry work in the vineyard of God where these gifts are given to bring the saints in to the fullness of Christ and in accordance to the life of God.

And he gave some, apostles; and some, prophets; and some, evangelists; and some, pastors and teachers; For the perfecting of the saints, for the work of the ministry, for the edifying of the body of Christ: Till we all come in the unity of the faith, and of the knowledge of the Son of God, unto a perfect man, unto the measure of the stature of the fullness of Christ: That we henceforth be no more children, tossed to and fro, and carried about with every wind of doctrine, by the sleight of men, and cunning craftiness, whereby they lie in wait to deceive; But speaking the truth in love may grow up into him in all things, which is the head, even Christ: From whom the whole body fitly joined together and compacted by that which every joint supplied, according to the effectual working in the measure of every part, maketh increase of the body unto the edifying of itself in love. This I say therefore, and testify in the Lord, that ye henceforth walk not as other Gentiles walk, in the vanity of their mind, Having the understanding darkened, being alienated from the life of God through the ignorance that is in them, because of the blindness of their heart. (Ephesians 4:11-18)

Camels were used to transport beauty, spices, and gold across the desert and roam in the desert to search for food and store up fat in humps for times of lack.

Camels depend very much on God for their provision of food.

John the Baptist used camel skin for his clothing and chose the desert as his place of manifestation of his ministry. We can see in the life of John the Baptist the major four characters to build in the mindset of godly character.

Endurance

The ability to stay on though suffering is apparent and difficulties are involved in a giving context or situation. Only the Word of God can build the spirit of endurance within us so as to avoid the temptation of giving up before accomplishing purpose and destiny. Knowing the outcome before engaging in a project helps to endure in the face of challenges.

Declaring the end from the beginning, and from ancient times the things that are not yet done, saying, my counsel shall stand, and I will do all my pleasure: Calling a ravenous bird from the east, the man that executes my counsel from a far country: yea, I have spoken it, I will also bring it to pass; I have purposed it, I will also do it. (Isaiah 46:10-11)

Having in mind that God is involved, victory is sure.

Endurance is to continue in the same state without giving up, and to suffer without resistance under pressure or pain.

Endurance is to support a situation without breaking out.

The voice of one crying in the wilderness, Prepare ye the way of the Lord, make his paths straight. John did baptize in the wilderness, and preach the baptism of repentance for the remission of sins. And there went out unto him all the land of Judaea, and they of Jerusalem, and were all baptized of him in the river of Jordan, confessing their sins. And John was clothed with camel's hair and with a girdle of a skin about his loins; and he did eat locusts and wild honey; And preached, saying, There cometh one mightier than I after me, the latchet of whose shoes I am not worthy to stoop down and unloose. (Mark 1:3-7)

Crying in the wilderness is a picture of extreme sorrow for the situations at hand. Baptism is the confession of a good conscience toward God, but just the first affirmation is an oath to say, "Yes Lord, I am ready to swim in the river of true life."

Eating locusts and honey is a clear picture of fasting, which is abstinence and the practice of fasting needs endurance, and with the help of the Holy Spirit, we can find the right balance in the period of fasting.

Putting on clothes made of camel hair was clear identification with the nature of the camel.

Tolerance:

A disposition to be indulgent toward those whose opinions or practices differ from one's own, not to judge or condemn with bigotry (Home study Dictionary Peal Press). "Unreasoning zeal, without understanding and dogmatism" (Home study Dictionary Peal Press).

And they came unto John, and said unto him, Rabbi, he that was with thee beyond Jordan, to whom thou barest witness, behold, the same baptized, and all men come to him. John answered and said, A man can receive nothing, except it be given him from heaven. Ye yourselves bear me witness that I said; I am not the Christ, but that I am sent before him. John 3:26-28

John was a rabbi, meaning a teacher, and he gives us clear understanding on the operation of tolerance, knowing that all have the right to knowledge.

Galatians 6:3: "For if a man thinks himself to be something, when he is nothing, he deceived himself."

Tolerance will always say, "Let it be known God is in control and with the power of intercession it's possible to change things."

Tolerance is not approval of wrong doing, but finding a solution in face of wrong doing through the power of the Holy Spirit by intercessory prayers.

Patience:

The character or habit of mind that enables one to suffer afflictions, provocation or other evil, with a calm unruffled temper; composure; quietness or calmness in waiting for some change to happen.

Be patient therefore, brethren, unto the coming of the Lord. Behold, the husbandman waiteth for the precious fruit of the earth, and hath long patience for it, until he receive the early and latter rain. Be ye also patient; establish your hearts: for the coming of the Lord draweth nigh. Grudge not one against another, brethren, lest ye be condemned: behold, the judge standeth before the door. Take, my brethren, the prophets, who have spoken in the name of the Lord, for an example of suffering affliction, and of patience. (James 5:7-10)

"Behold, we count them happy which endure. Ye have heard of the patience of Job, and have seen the end of the Lord; that the Lord is very pitiful, and of tender mercy." (James 5:11)

Humility:

John answered and said, "A man can receive nothing, except it be

given him from heaven. Ye yourselves bear me witness that I said
I am not the Christ, but that I am
sent before him. He that hath
the bride is the bridegroom: but
the friend of the bridegroom,
which standeth and heareth
him, rejoiceth greatly because
of the bridegroom's voice: this
my joy therefore is fulfilled."
(John 3:27-30)

He must increase, but I must decrease.
The camel will always go down to
carry load and at the service without
any reserve ready to follow commands
of others.

"He gives to the beast his food,
and to the young ravens which
cry. He delighted not in the

strength of the horse: he takes not pleasure in the legs of a man. The Lord takes pleasure in them that fear him, in those that hope in his mercy." (Psalm 147:9-11)

The woman who fears the Lord shall be praised.

The character of the woman was to be measured by her service, both to the helper and to the camels, according to the prayers that Elizer will offer unto God.

And he made his camels to kneel down without the city by a well of water at the time of the evening, even the time that women go out to draw water. And he said, "O Lord God of my master Abraham, I pray thee, send me good speed this day, and shew kindness unto my master Abraham. Behold, I stand here by the well of water; and the daughters of the men of the city come out to draw water: And let it come to pass, that the damsel to whom I shall say, 'Let down thy pitcher, I pray thee, that I may drink;' and she shall say, 'Drink, and I will give thy camels drink also: let the same be she that thou hast appointed for thy servant Isaac; and thereby shall I know that thou hast showed kindness unto my master.'" And it came to pass, before he had done speaking, that, behold, Rebecca came out, who was born to Bethuel, son of Milcah, the wife of Nahor, Abraham's brother, with her pitcher upon her shoulder. And the damsel was very fair to look upon, a virgin, neither had any man known her: and she went down to the well, and filled her pitcher, and came up. And the servant ran to meet her, and said, "Let me, I pray thee, drink a little water of thy pitcher." And she said, "Drink, my lord: and she hasted, and let down her pitcher upon her hand, and gave him drink." And when she had done giving him drink, she said, "I will draw water for thy camels also, until they have done drinking." And she hasted, and emptied her pitcher into the trough, and ran again unto the well to draw water, and drew for all his camels. And the man wondering at her held his peace, to wit whether the Lord had made his journey prosperous or not. And it came to pass, as the camels had done drinking, that the man took a golden earring of half a shekel weight, and two bracelets for her hands of ten shekels weight of gold. (Genesis 24:11-22)

> Verily I say unto you, "It shall be more tolerable for the land of Sodom and Gomorrah in the day of judgment, than for that

city." Behold, I send you forth as sheep in the midst of wolves: be ye therefore wise as serpents, and harmless as doves. But beware of men: for they will deliver you up to the councils, and they will scourge you in their synagogues; And ye shall be brought before governors and kings for my sake, for a testimony against them and the Gentiles. But when they deliver you up, take no thought how or what ye shall speak: for it shall be given that same hour what ye shall speak. For it is not ye that speak, but the Spirit of your Father which speaketh in you. And the brother shall deliver up the brother to death, and the father the child: and the children shall rise up against their parents, and cause them to be put to death. And ye shall be hated of all men for my name's sake: but he that endured to the end shall be saved. But when they persecute you in this city, flee ye into another: for verily I say unto you, "Ye shall not have gone over the cities of Israel, till the Son of man become. The disciple is not above his master, nor the servant above his lord." It is enough for the disciple that he be as his master, and the servant as his lord. If they have called the master of the house Beelzebub, how much more shall they call them of his household? Fear them not therefore: for there is nothing covered, that shall not be revealed; and hid, that shall not be known. What I tell you in darkness, that speaks ye in light: and what ye hear in the ear, that preach ye upon the housetops. And fear not them which kill the body, but are not able to kill the soul: but rather fear him which is able to destroy both soul and body in hell. Are not two sparrows sold for a farthing? And one of them shall not fall on the ground without your Father. But the very hairs of your head are all numbered. Fear ye not therefore, ye are of more value than many sparrows. Whosoever therefore shall confess me before men, him will I confess also before my Father which is in heaven. But whosoever shall deny me before men, him will I also deny before my Father which is in heaven.

Think not that I am come to send peace on earth: I came not to send peace, but a sword. For I am come to set a man at variance against his father, and the daughter against her mother, and the daughter in law against her mother in law. And a man's foes shall be they of his own household. He that loves father or mother more than me is not worthy of me: and he that loves son or daughter more than me is not worthy of me. And he that takes not his cross, and followed after me, is not worthy of me. He that fined his life shall lose it: and he that loses his life for my sake shall find it. He that receives you receives me, and he that receives me receives him that sent me. He that receives a prophet in the name of a prophet shall receive a prophet's reward; and he that receives a righteous man in the name of a righteous man shall receive a righteous man's reward. And whosoever shall give to drink unto one of these little ones a cup of cold water only in the name of a disciple, verily I say unto you, he shall in no wise lose his reward. (Matthew 10:15-42)

Conditions in the desert can be overcome with the power of endurance and Rebecca was to be tested in supplying water for ten camels and for the master of the camel. She willingly rendered her service with any thought behind her mind. Destiny encounters are never prepared for. The willingness to serve comes out of the gain inside of the one giving opportunity to serve. She responded to her destiny encounter without any constraint. She endured to supply ten camels with water and generosity extend to offer shelter to a stranger who held the key of her liberation, the one who will carry her to the place where her laughter waited.

> Looking unto Jesus the author and finisher of our faith; who for the joy that was set before him endured the cross, despising the shame, and is set down at the right hand of the throne of God. For consider him that endured such contradiction of sinners against himself, lest ye be wearied and faint in your minds. (Hebrews 12:2-3)

The Character Structure of Rebecca's Family:

Nahor -uncle & husband to milkah	Bethuel -son of milkah and Nahor- who later become father to Laban and Rebecca	Milkah
	Laban	Rebecca

And it came to pass, before he had done speaking, that, behold, Rebecca came out, who was born to Bethel, son of Milcah, the wife of Nahor, Abraham's brother, with her pitcher upon her shoulder. And the damsel was very fair to look upon, a virgin, neither had any man known her: and she went down to the well, and filled her pitcher, and came up.

She was daughter of Bethuel, whose name signifies waste or desolation or destroying of God, which is not a surprise because it's from this background that Abraham was called and the father of Bethel stayed back in Mesopotamia.

On the other hand, the mother is Milcah, which is the feminine for Meleck, which means "king" and therefore Milcah means, "queen."

The name of the grandfather is not left out, which is Nahor, and has a meaning, "snore," as in sleeping.

We also have his brother who is called Laban with meaning interestingly contrasted to his character. The meaning is "white."

The Foolishness of God is Wiser

Because the foolishness of God is wiser than men; and the weakness of God is stronger than men. For ye see your calling, brethren, how that not many wise men after the flesh, not many mighty, not many noble, are called: But God hath chosen the foolish things of the world to confound the wise; and God hath chosen the weak things of the world to confound the things which are mighty; And base things of the world, and things which are despised, hath God chosen, yea, and things which are not, to bring to naught things that are: That no flesh should glory in his presence. But of him are ye in Christ Jesus, who of God is made unto us wisdom, and righteousness, and sancti-fication, and redemption: That, according as it is written, "He that

gloried, let him glory in the Lord."
1 Corinthians 1:25-31

One whose legs are tied, born by a character whose name is desolation who is issuer of one who is known for his snoring sleep and having a brother whose character composition in light to his name speaks of nothing but hypocrisy with the only spectrum of hope related to the mother whose name is identify to a queen, can only trust to the power of the Holy Spirit for the liberation of her destiny.

Ephesians 5:14-16: "Wherefore he saith, 'Awake thou that sleeps, and arise from the dead, and Christ shall give you light. See then that ye walk circumspectly, not as fools, but as wise, redeeming the time, because the days are evil.'"

Family dysfunction is healed by the bond of oath to bring about rules and regulations.

Now these are the generations of Terah: Terah begat Abram, Nahor, and Haran; and Haran begat Lot. And Haran died before his father Terah in the land of his nativity, in Ur of the Chaldees. And Abram and Nahor took them wives: the name of Abram's wife was Sarai; and the name of Nahor's wife, Milcah, the daughter of Haran, the father of Milcah, and the father of Iscah. But Sarai was barren; she had no child. And Terah took Abram his son, and Lot the son of Haran his son's son, and Sarai his daughter in law, his son Abram's wife; and they went forth with them from Ur of the Chaldees, to go into the land of Canaan; and they came unto Haran, and dwelt there. And the days of Terah were two hundred and five years: and Terah died in Haran. (Genesis 11:27-32)

Abraham

Haran father of Lot , **Milcah & Iscah**

Nahor uncle of Milcah & later on husband . Sons of Milkah, Huz,Buz,kemuel, Chesed,Hazo,Pil dash,Jidlaph and Bethuel With concubine Reumah who gave him four sons Tebah,Gaham, thahash & Maachah.

Terah the Father

Sarah Daughter & Daughter inlaw

And it came to pass after these things, that it was told Abraham, saying, "Behold, Milcah, she hath also born children unto thy brother Nahor; Huz his first-born, and Buz his brother, and Kemuel the father of Aram, And Chesed, and Hazo, and Pildash, and Jidlaph, and Bethuel. And Bethuel begat Rebekah: these eight Milcah did bear to Nahor, Abraham's brother. And his concubine, whose name was Reumah, she bare also Tebah, and Gaham, and Thahash, and Maachah." (Genesis 22:20-24)

Chapter Four:

Mindset of Well Doing

And she said, "Drink, my lord: and she hasted, and let down her pitcher upon her hand, and gave him drink." And when she had done giving him drink, she said, "I will draw water for thy camels also, until they have done drinking." And she hasted, and emptied her pitcher into the trough, and ran again unto the well to draw water, and drew for all his camels. And the man wondering at her held his peace, to wit whether the LORD had made his journey prosperous or not. And it came to pass, as the camels had done drinking, that the man took a golden earring of half a shekel weight, and two bracelets for her hands of ten shekels weight of gold. (Genesis 24:18-22)

To clog by tying the fetlock, Rebecca is opening her way up the part of her destiny with voluntary service to a stranger who, in his peace, is preparing precious gift that will bring more physical color to her already complimented beauty. The response of the demand for what bore more willingness to do more and little did she understand, it was a response to a prayer that was the desire of the heart of righteous Abraham.

Her generosity and liberality will attract gold, a beautiful woman kept aside her beauty in other to serve water to a stranger and ten camels.

She was a virgin, she was beautiful, and above all she was a servant; rendering service unto men as unto God is a key to breakthrough.

She ran to serve; something in her setup moved her to render service to her destiny helper without knowing, Eliezer was at peace and contemplated the response of his prayer according to the God of Abraham.

When there is a servant to pray, God will always be willing to do according to His good pleasure.

"For it is God which worked in you both to will and to do of his good pleasure." (Philippians 2:13)

"But my God shall supply all your need according to his riches in glory by Christ Jesus." (Philippians 4:19)

"Now unto God and our Father be glory forever and ever. Amen." (Philippians 4:20)

And let the peace of God rule in your hearts, to which also ye are called in one body; and be ye thankful. Let the word of Christ dwell in you richly in all wisdom; teaching and admonishing one another in psalms and hymns and spiritual songs, singing with grace in your hearts to the Lord. And whatsoever ye do in word or deed, do all in the name of the Lord Jesus, giving thanks

to God and the Father by him.
(Colossians 3:15-17)

Mindset of doing well never comes
by chance; it applies action and observa-
tion. On one hand, we see how sponta-
neous Rebecca was in rendering service:
she ran to fetch water both for the servants and for ten camels while the servant observed to see the unfolding of
the will of God through the well doing
of the lady. She gives a sense of urgency
in the act of running because ten camels'
capacity of drinking is not a light thing
to do; it entails effort and dispensing
of energy.

Her service to the servants and the
camels was her service to God. She supplied the need of the camels and the men,
thus allowing God to work through her,
fulfilling the Word of God as seen in the

words of Apostle Paul: "For it is God which works in you both to will and to do of his good pleasure. But my God shall supply all your need according to his riches in glory by Christ Jesus."

A Mindset of Well Doing is a Kingdom Mindset Principle

Rebecca was single and not thinking about marriage, but her well doing attracted supply of a future need. When the due season has come, nothing can stop it except the lack of well doing. If we do well in every opportunity without any gain, well doing will be attracting the manifestation of a need in due season.

"And let us not be weary in well doing: for in due season we shall reap, if we faint not. As we have therefore opportunity, let us do well unto all *men,* especially unto them who are of the household of faith." (Galatians 6:9-10)

"Therefore, my beloved brethren, be ye steadfast, unmovable, always abounding in the work of the Lord, forasmuch as ye know that your labour is not in vain in the Lord." (1 Corinthians 15:58)

"But ye, brethren, be not weary in well doing." (2 Thessalonians 3:13)

"To them who by patient continuance in well doing seek for glory and honor and immortality, eternal life." (Romans 2:7)

"For so is the will of God, that with well doing ye may put to silence

the ignorance of foolish men." (1
Peter 2:15)

"For *it is* better, if the will of God
be so, that ye suffer for well doing,
than for evil doing." (1 Peter 3:17)_

A Mindset of Well Doing Opens Doors
for Promotion

In the year 1998, in the city of Bamenda
in the northwest region of Cameroon, the
regional delegate of tourism came to my
house while a Campus for Christ evan-
gelism team stayed in my house and met
a situation of illness of my child and took
the child to the general hospital, paid for
the drugs, and all the charges.

Upon my arrival from my trip, which
I did to go and prayed for the director
of political affairs at the ministry of ter-
ritorial administration who was ill of a

terminal disease after my prayers for him, he was instantly healed and his health was restored back to normal.

As I came back, the information was given to me of the situation of the child who was sick in my house and how the delegate intervenes, then I decided to say thank you to the delegate in his office.

As we talked about several issuers, then it was time to pray and I asked him, "Sir, what will you like God to do for you in return for this kindness you did for me?"

He said, "I want God to grant me the possibility to be transferred to my region of origin, seeing he is getting to the age of retirement."

I proceeded and asked, "What is the highest position of ranking in your ministry?"

He responded, "That of a minister."

Then I said, "Now hear the Word of the Lord. You shall be promoted above the rank of the minister," and he said, "Amen."

One month later, a presidential decree came out declaring him the central African representative for tourism in the European Union with offices in Paris and Brussels. That is what God can do when we give our heart to the mindset of well doing.

Some years later, I met with the delegate in the city of Paris, France and we talked about these things and recounted on the goodness of God and all the wonderful things He did for us. Whenever there is opportunity to do good or render service to fellow man, just do it and know God is forever present and keeps records of our acts of kindness.

A Mindset of Well-doing Opens the Door for Financial Prosperity

"And it came to pass, as the camels had done drinking, that the man took a golden earring of half a shekel weight, and two bracelets for her hands of ten shekels weight of gold." (Genesis 24:22)

In the year 2004, I was in front of a rented property we had to run our Bible institute in the city of Douala, Cameroon and I saw two heavy trucks passing by and making a turn. A few minutes later, they returned to my direction and stopped at my courtyard. A man stepped down, greeted me, and asked for permission to use our yard to unload the trucks. They had been looking for a place in the city to unload, but no one was willing to grant them space.

I told him to go ahead and use the field in front of the property, and he was excited. Then he asked for a glass of water, and I invited him in to the main hall. He noticed our single computer on the sectary's table and asked me what we use computers for, and I told him our administration and Bible school. He told me he had a dozen of them in the truck from Canada and that we could have them all for free.

"A mindset of well doing is a platform for hospitality." (Genesis 24:23)

"And said, 'Whose daughter art thou? Tell me, I pray thee: is there room in thy father's house for us to lodge in?'" (Genesis 24:24)

"And she said unto him, 'I am the daughter of Bethuel the

son of Milcah, which she bare unto Nahor.'"

"She said moreover unto him, we have both straw and provender enough, and room to lodge in." (Genesis 24:25)

Later, my unexpected guest from Canada asked for room in the center for the night. I said it was not a comfortable place for him, but he said as long as it's a place where the Word of God is thought and prayers are offered up to God, he, being a non-believer, would prefer to sleep in this place rather than going to a hotel.

We offered him a place, and from there he carried out all his business transactions. When it was time for him to go back to Canada, he gave us the five cars that were left unsold out of the containers for free, just for the simple well doing rendered unto a stranger.

A Mindset of Well-doing Creates an Atmosphere of Worship

> "And the man bowed down his head, and worshipped the Lord." (Genesis 24:26)

> "And he said, 'Blessed be the Lord God of my master Abraham, who hath not left destitute my master of his mercy and his truth: I being in the way, the Lord led me to the house of my master's brethren.'" (Genesis 24:27)

"And the damsel ran, and told them of her mother's house these things." (Genesis 24:28)

"And Rebecca had a brother, and his name was Laban: and Laban ran out unto the man, unto the well." (Genesis 24:29)

"And it came to pass, when he saw the earring and bracelets upon his sister's hands, and when he heard the words of Rebecca his sister, saying, 'Thus space the man unto me; that he came unto the man; and, behold, he stood by the camels at the well.'" (Genesis 24:30)

The true worshippers shall worship the Father in spirit and in truth: for the Father seeketh such to worship him.

"There cometh a woman of Samaria to draw water: Jesus saith unto her, 'Give me to drink.'" (John 4:7)

"For his disciples were gone away unto the city to buy meat." (John 4:8)

"Then saith the woman of Samaria unto him, 'How is it that thou, being a Jew, ask drink of me, which am a woman of Samaria? For the Jews have no dealings with the Samaritans.'" (John 4:9)

"Jesus answered and said unto her, 'If thou knewest the gift of God, and who it is that saith to thee, "Give me to drink;" thou wouldest have asked of him, and he would have given thee living water.'" (John 4:10)

"The woman saith unto him, 'Sir, thou hast nothing to draw with, and the well is deep: from whence then hast thou that living water?'" (John 4:11)

"Art thou greater than our father Jacob, which gave us the well, and drank thereof himself, and his children, and his cattle?" (John 4:12)

"Jesus answered and said unto her, 'Whosoever drinketh of this water shall thirst again.'" (John 4:13)

"But whosoever drinketh of the water that I shall give him shall never thirst; but the water that I shall give him shall be in him a well of water springing up into everlasting life." (John 4:14)

"The woman saith unto him, 'Sir, give me this water, that I thirst not, neither come hither to draw.'" (John 4:15)

"Jesus saith unto her, 'Go, call thy husband, and come hither.'" (John 4:16)

"The woman answered and said, 'I have no husband.' Jesus said unto her, 'Thou hast well said, "I have no husband."'" (John 4:17)

"For thou hast had five husbands; and he whom thou now hast is not thy husband: in that saidst thou truly." (John 4:18)

"The woman saith unto him, 'Sir, I perceive that thou art a prophet.'" (John 4:19)

"Our fathers worshipped in this mountain; and ye say, that in Jerusalem is the place where men ought to worship." (John 4:20)

"Jesus saith unto her, 'Woman, believe me, the hour cometh,

when ye shall neither in this mountain, nor yet at Jerusalem, worship the Father.'" (John 4:21)

"Ye worship ye know not what: we know what we worship: for salvation is of the Jews." (John 4:22)

"But the hour cometh and now is, when the true worshippers shall worship the Father in spirit and in truth: for the Father seeketh such to worship him." (John 4:23)

"God is a Spirit: and they that worship him must worship him in spirit and in truth." (John 4:24)

Key Elements for a Life of Worship

Mercy and truth are the key elements for a life of worship. It's only a merciful and truthful heart that God responds to in an atmosphere of worship. Without mercy and truth, worship is vain. The woman coming to the well to meet the master understood that worship exists and that her people worship on the mountain while Jews do theirs in Jerusalem. She knew the facts, but lacked the knowledge of the truth, and that is the case with many people.

Unlike Rebecca, she was a sinner living in her lost state, but needed the mercy of God without knowing that in front of her was the living God asking for water. Rebecca was a virgin who knew no man, but her name was a great hindrance; her service become her key to open up the treasures of heaven on her behalf. Her kindness was an expression of mercy.

Worship is a state of being revealed through kind services rendered to fellow man it is a part of our spirit man; that is why Jesus said it is to be done in truth and in spirit.

"Let not mercy and truth forsake thee: bind them about thy neck; write them upon the table of thine heart: So shall thou find favour and good understanding in the sight of God and man." (Proverbs 3:3-4)

"By mercy and truth iniquity is purged: and by the fear of the Lord men depart from evil." (Proverbs 20:28)

"Mercy and truth preserve the king: and his throne is upholden by mercy." (Proverbs 16:6)

"All the paths of the Lord are mercy and truth unto such as keep his covenant and his testimonies." (Psalm 25:10)

"For the law was given by Moses, but grace and truth came by Jesus Christ." (John 1:17)

Chapter Five

The Mindset of Humility

Humility is the ability to consent from one state to another and the capacity to be empathetic in service toward fellow man. The mindset of humility puts first things first and takes to heart the interest of others.

Upon arrival, Eliezer was offered food, but he chose to stick to the purpose for which he was sent. He ignored his appetite until he delivered that for which he was sent; he cautiously presented his master and identified himself as a servant.

The Mindset of Humility is the Mind of Christ

> Let this mind be in you, which was also in Christ Jesus: Who, being in the form of God, thought it not robbery to be equal with God: But made himself of no reputation, and took upon him the form of a servant, and was made in the likeness of men: And being found in fashion as a man, he humbled himself, and became obedient unto death, even the death of the cross. (Philippians 2:5-8)

Reputation has become a serious problem amongst the people of God and in this end time, everyone wants to be identifying with the titles that are giving to the ministry gift of apostle, prophet, evangelist, pastor, and teacher. Most often those identifying with the titles don't even represent the virtues and characteristics that goes with the titles.

"But made him of no reputation, and took upon him the form of a servant, and was made in the likeness of men." (Genesis 24:31-32)

The Mindset of Humility Opens Closed Doors

"And he said, 'Come in, thou blessed of the Lord; wherefore standest thou without? For I have prepared the house, and room for the camels.'"

And the man came into the house: and he unguarded his camels, and gave straw and provender for the camels, and water to wash his feet, and the men's feet that were with him.

He was given a place in the house because he was part of the body by the oath taken with his master, we are the body of Christ the temple of the Holy Spirit who comes in and dwells with us, the Holy Spirit is to be invited in and lives inside in our heart to come and soup with us.

"What? Know ye not that your body is the temple of the Holy Ghost which is in you, which ye have of God, and ye are not your own?" (1 Corinthians 6:19)

Because of the oath with his master, he became blessed of the lord. We form part of the body of the household of God; we are not to be exclusive, but inclusive.

The Mindset of Humility Creates Room for Others

The camel had also a place prepared for them. As we have seen before, the

camel is a typical representation of servanthood, having temperance, endurance,
and patience, where humility is found
in the other virtues. In the same way a
camel stoops down to lift up people and
goods, humility goes before elevation.

Humility is the demonstration of
servanthood.

> So after he had washed their feet,
> and had taken his garments, and
> was set down again, he said unto
> them, "Know ye what I have
> done to you? Ye call me Master
> and Lord: and ye say well; for
> so I am. If I then, your Lord and
> Master, have washed your feet;
> ye also ought to wash one anoth-
> er's feet. For I have given you an
> example, that ye should do as I

have done to you. Verily, verily, I say unto you, the servant is not greater than his lord; neither had he that is sent greater than he that sent him. If ye know these things, happy are ye if ye do them. I speak not of you all: I know whom I have chosen: but that the scripture may be fulfilled, He that eateth bread with me hath lifted up his heel against me. Now I tell you before it come, that, when it is come to pass, ye may believe that I am he. Verily, verily, I say unto you, He that receives whomsoever I send receives me; and he that receives me receives him that sent me." (John 13:12-20)

The Mindset of Humility Indicates When to Eat

"Woe to thee, O land, when thy king is a child, and thy princes eat in the morning! Blessed art thou, O land, when thy king is the son of nobles, and thy princes eat in due season, for strength, and not for drunkenness!" (Ecclesiastes 10:16 -17)

Nobility is a product of humility and generosity is the display of nobility. Eating in the morning is symbolic for early gratifications, which is consumption without production. Some people don't wait for the appointed time for a project to yield before tempering with profit.

And there was set meat before him to eat: but he said, "I will not eat, until I have told mine errand." And he said, "Speak on." And he said, "I am Abraham's servant. And the Lord hath blessed my master greatly; and he is become great: and he hath given him flocks, and herds, and silver, and gold, and menservants, and maidservants, and camels, and asses. And Sarah my master's wife bare a son to my master when she was old: and unto him hath he given all that he hath. And my master made me swears, saying, 'Thou shall not take a wife to my son of the daughters of the Canaanites, in whose land I dwell:' but thou shall go unto my father's house, and to my kindred, and take a wife unto my son. And I said unto my master, 'Peradventure the woman will not follow me.' And he said unto me, 'The Lord, before whom I walk, will send his angel with thee, and prosper thy way; and thou shall take a wife for my son of my kindred, and of my father's house:' Then shall thou be clear from this my oath, when thou comest to my kindred; and if they give not thee one, thou shall be clear from my oath. (Genesis 24:33-41)

Humility is Rooted in the Fear of the Lord

The fear of the LORD is to hate evil: pride, and arrogance, and the evil way, and the forward mouth, do I hate. Counsel is mine, and sound wisdom: I am understanding; I have strength. By me kings reign, and princes decree justice. By me princes rule, and nobles, even all the judges of the earth. I love them that love me; and those that seek me early shall find me. (Proverbs 8:13-18)

Humility is the way to Honor

"The fear of the Lord is the instruction of wisdom, and before honor is humility." (Proverbs 15:33)

Rebecca ran several times to the well to fetch for water to quench the test of ten camels. She was beautiful, pure, and was not of any obligation to render service to a stranger. Many people are unable to grab certain opportunities just for the sake of pride and prejudice. Some consider their status and are unable to mixed with strangers and society. They form classes and sphere of influence and if you are not in their community, then you can't relate with them. Rebecca responded to a stranger and that was the starting point to get her husband through this stranger whom she offered her generosity and service.

Humility is the way of wisdom.

> "Before destruction the heart of man is haughty, and before honor is humility." (Proverbs 18:12)

In the year 1998, at the Full Gospel Bible Institute, Bamenda Nkwen, a young student, took permission to go out of campus for shopping on a day set aside for manual labor. Upon arrival, the labor prefect of the school asked why this young man was not present for the regular clean up of the campus. He responded to the prefect with proof of permission granted to him by the general prefect of the institution, who was in charge for warranting permission.

The labor prefect rejected the permission and said the young man would be punished. The young man protested and notified the general prefect who, instead of applying the rules, decided to agree to the punishment. The young man took the matter to the school authorities, who also refused to give consideration. Since the young man objected, the punishment was added and for seven days, he was to clean the toilets of the school. The young man knew he was right, but injustice prevailed over justice in a Bible school, which is the seat of righteousness.

Day after day he did his duty. During this time, a new governing board was elected to run the disciplinary structure of the school. The young man was nominated amongst three other candidates. They went through voting and the young man won. When asked what his motto was for the new disciplinary board he said, "Diligence, discipline, and devotion." Even through an unjust situation, humility worked in his life and he concluded humility is not only to be humble, but it also implies being diligent, devoted, and disciplined. In most of the culture in my native Cameroon, we have people who are serving in the courts of our chiefs and are called nobles. This is a prestigious title by demonstration of positive contribution in the local community by working diligently and showing a great sense of engagement in the village activities.

Another factor that grant this illustrious title is discipline in family and public life. In light of these three characteristics, one is termed humble and is chosen to be noble.

> "For thus saith the high and lofty One that inhabited eternity, whose name is Holy; I dwell in the high and holy place, with him also that is of a contrite and humble spirit, to revive the spirit of the humble, and to revive the heart of the contrite ones." (Isaiah 57:15)

The Mindset of Humility is a Choice

He humbled Himself and became obedient unto death, even the death of the cross. Our Lord and Savior Jesus Christ condescended to take our position of condemnation in exchange that we should become like him in the sight of God.

> "Sacrifice and offering thou didst not desire; mine ears hast thou opened: burnt offering and sin offering hast thou not required." (Psalm 40:6)

> "Then said I, 'Lo, I come: in the volume of the book it is written of me.'" (Psalm 40:7)

> "I delight to do thy will, O my God: yea, thy law is within my heart." (Psalm 40:8)

"I have preached righteousness in
the great congregation: lo, I have
not refrained my lips, O Lord,
thou knowest." (Psalm 40:9)

"I have not hid thy righteousness
within my heart; I have declared
thy faithfulness and thy salvation: I have not concealed thy
loving-kindness and thy truth
from the great congregation."
(Psalm 40:10)

Willingness and selflessness is
important to build the mindset of
humility so as to be in line with destiny
encounter, which is an expression of
fulfilling the mind of God. Christ Jesus,
in His writing was slain even before
the foundation of the earth and came
according to the set time of God to set

mankind free. In like manner, for us to be in turn with our destiny encounter, we must follow His example having the same mind that was in Him.

The Mindset of Humility is the Mark of Stewardship

The mindset of humility is the mark of true stewardship, this is the mark Eliezer achieved in the house of his master Abraham, to the point of him considering him to be the heir of his inheritance, except for the intervention of God. Humility is important to build in the life of people and our personal lives. It is the ability to adapt in changing circumstances of life and keeping once real composure with dignity, even in the face of adversity. This can only be true when we are submitted to a higher authority. I have come to note in this life that only nobles can be humble because humility has its root from nobility. Christ Jesus is the perfect example of this (Philippians 2:6-8).

God is the initiator of any encounter of destiny and one of His criteria for us is a to have a mindset of humility.

> "And Abram said, 'Lord God, what wilt thou give me, seeing I go childless, and the steward of my house is this Eliezer of Damascus?'" (Genesis 15:2)

The way up is through the way down and the way down is through the way up.

There is no causality for encounters of destiny because they are designed and programmed by God for the purpose of profitability for those involved and for the kingdom of God.

The person you neglect up the hill might be the one you need when on the way coming back down the hill because everything that goes up will still come down, and that which goes around will still come around. As a potter takes the clay and gives it a form of beauty, so to God takes a life that is surrendered to him to design it and give it a form directed by his thought in the step of Destiny encounter.

Tabernacle Foundation Publishing

Fritz Takang
Founder
Tabernacle Foundation International
Touching lives in the nations of the earth.

www.ingramcontent.com/pod-product-compliance
Lightning Source LLC
Chambersburg PA
CBHW030623060526
44539CB00042B/726